New Dimensions
IN THE
WORLD OF READING

ALL THROUGH THE TOWN

P R O G R A M   A U T H O R S

James F. Baumann	Roselmina Indrisano	P. David Pearson
Theodore Clymer	Dale D. Johnson	Taffy E. Raphael
Carl Grant	Connie Juel	Marian Davies Toth
Elfrieda H. Hiebert	Jeanne R. Paratore	Richard L. Venezky

Contributing Author: Rosann Englebretson

COVER
ILLUSTRATOR

Spotlight

Mark Buehner

☀ When artist Mark Buehner was in first grade, he liked make-believe. Now he draws funny make-believe animals.

☀ Some of his make-believe animals are on the cover of this book. The bright colors and the playful look of the animals make his artwork fun.

SILVER BURDETT GINN

NEEDHAM, MA   MORRISTOWN, NJ

ATLANTA, GA   DALLAS, TX   DEERFIELD, IL   MENLO PARK, CA

Theme

Here We Go!

Theme Books for
Here We Go!

If you like stories about wheels, here are some books you might enjoy.

✳ A loose wheel takes a bouncy, jumpy trip through town in *Wheel Away* by Dayle Ann Dodds. Will it ever stop?

✳ Thanks to wheels, trucks are always on the move. Read *Trucks* by Gail Gibbons to find out about all the things trucks do for us.

✳ In *Move It!* by Deborah Eaton, Big Wheel Movers move something that's pretty big, wide, and tall!

✳ Wheels help build a house in *Wood for a House* by Carl Murano. How many wheels can you find helping out?

✳ What's stopping the car in *I Wonder Why This Car Can't Go* by Maggie Goodrich? It's not the wheels!

✳ Read *A New Wheel* by Arthur Restham to find out how a family of hamsters gets a new wheel for their cage.

SING ALONG

The Wheels on the Bus

The wheels on the bus
go round and round,
round and round,
round and round.
The wheels on the bus
go round and round—
All through the town.

The people on the bus
go up and down,
up and down,
up and down.
The people on the bus
go up and down—
All through the town.

whose mouse are you?

BY ROBERT KRAUS • PICTURES BY JOSE ARUEGO

Whose mouse are you?

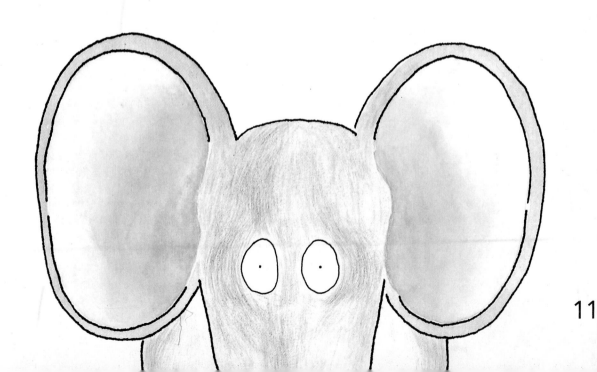

Nobody's mouse.

Where is your mother?

Inside the cat.

Where is your father?

Caught in a trap.

Where is your sister?

Far from home.

Where is your brother?

I have none.

What will you do?

Shake my mother out of the cat!

22

Free my father from the trap!

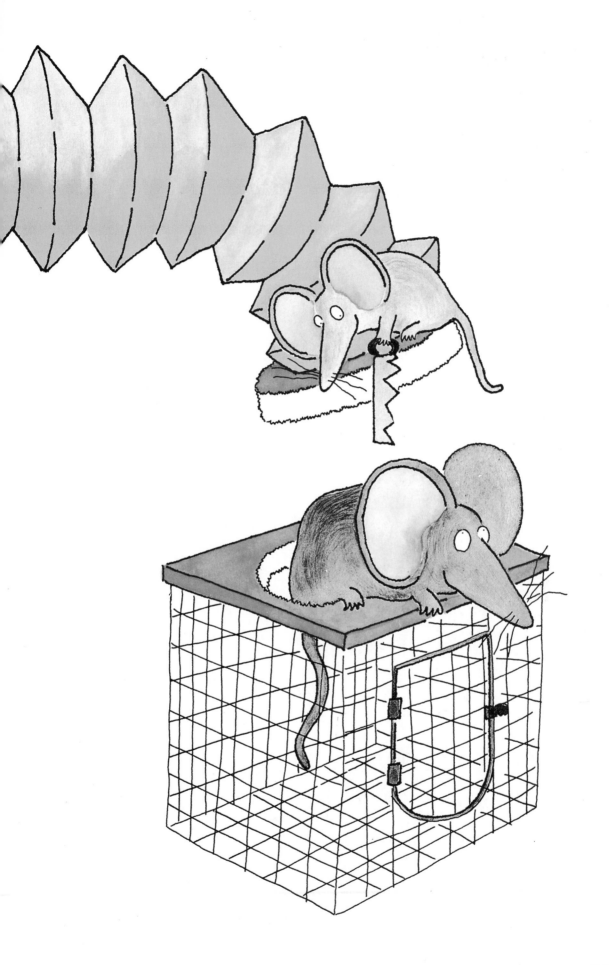

Find my sister and bring her home.

Wish for a brother as I have none.

Now whose mouse are you?

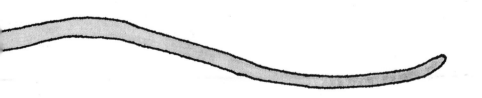

My mother's mouse, she loves me so.

My father's mouse, from head to toe.

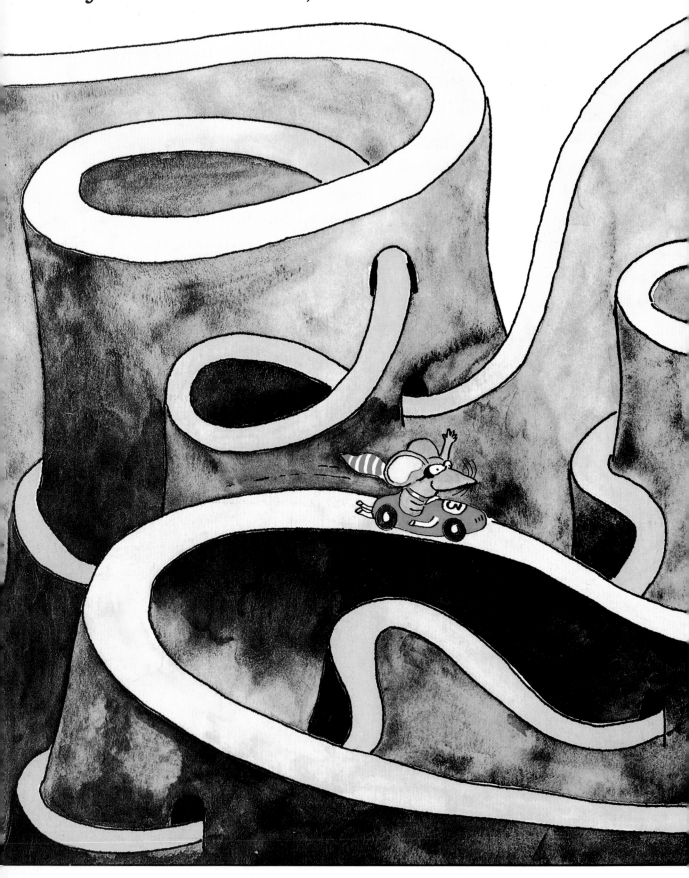

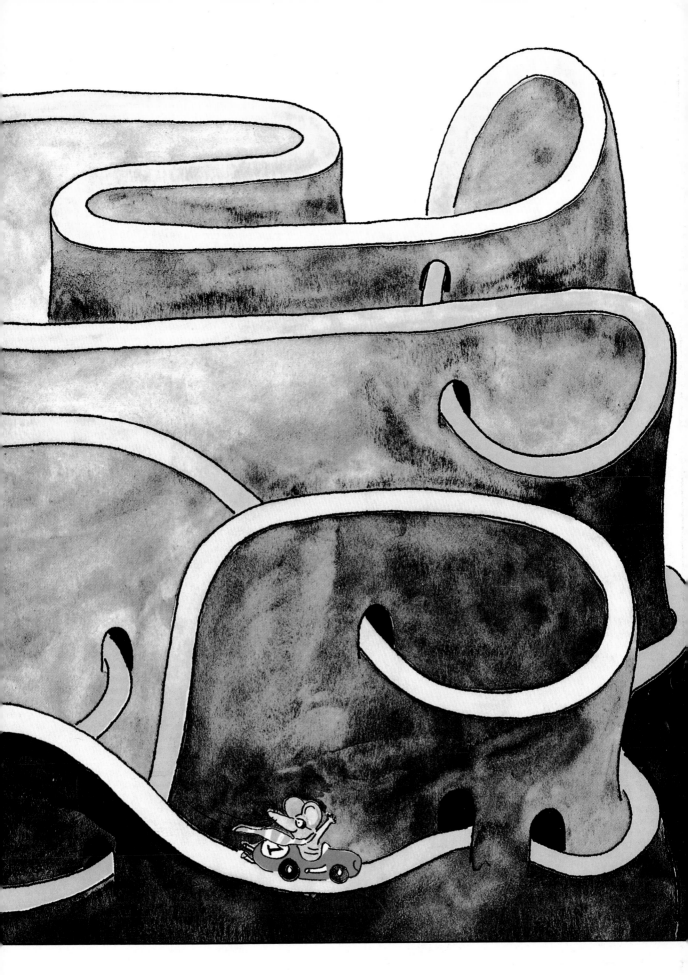

My sister's mouse, she loves me too.

My brother's mouse....

Your brother's mouse?

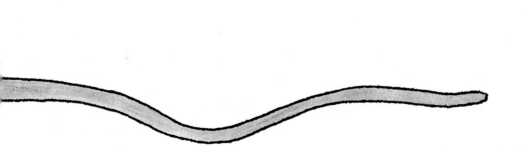

My brother's mouse—he's *brand* new!

by Katherine Mead illustrated by Tim Lee

TICKE

ALL ABOARD!

Click clack
Step back.
Train is chugging down the track.

Watch your step.
Here's a seat.

Click clack
Step back.
Train is chugging down the track.

44

Station stop.

Click clack
Step back.
Train is chugging down the track.

Home again.

Click clack
Step back.
Train is chugging down the track.

All Aboard!

Song of the Train

Clickety-clack,
Wheels on the track,
This is the way
They begin the attack:
Click-ety-clack,
Click-ety-clack,
Click-ety, *clack*-ety,
Click-ety
Clack.

Clickety-clack,
Over the crack,
Faster and faster
The song of the track:
Clickety-clack,
Clickety-clack,
Clickety, clackety,
Clackety.
Clack.

Riding in front,
Riding in back,
Everyone hears
The song of the track:
Clickety-clack,
Clickety-clack,
Clickety, *clickety*,
Clackety
Clack.

David McCord

Wheels

written by Christina Midori

illustrated by Karen Watson

Can you use wheels to work or play?
Can you use wheels every day?

You can use wheels to get to school.
Wheels on a bus,
Wheels on a car,
Wheels on a bike
if school is not far.

You can use wheels in the park.
Wheels on skates,
Wheels on a bike,
Wheels on a ride
if that's what you like.

You can use wheels all around.
Wheels to work and wheels to play,
You can use wheels every day.

Sing a Song of Subways

Sing a song of subways,
Never see the sun;
Four-and-twenty people
In room for one.

When the doors are opened—
Everybody run.

Eve Merriam

ACROSS THE STREAM

BY MIRRA GINSBURG

PICTURES BY NANCY TAFURI

A hen

and three chicks

had a
bad
dream.

They ran and came

to a
deep,
wide
stream.

The hen
said, "Cluck,
we are
in luck.

I see three ducklings

and a duck."

The duck was kind,
she did not mind.

She said, "Quack, get on my back."

They were in luck.
They crossed the stream—

a chick on a duckling,

a chick on a duckling,

a chick on a duckling,

and the hen on the duck.

And what became of

the bad dream?

It was left on the other
side of the stream.

WORDS

by Bill Martin Jr
and John Archambault

Some words are long words.

dinosaur

cafeteria

Some words are short words.

READ ALOUD

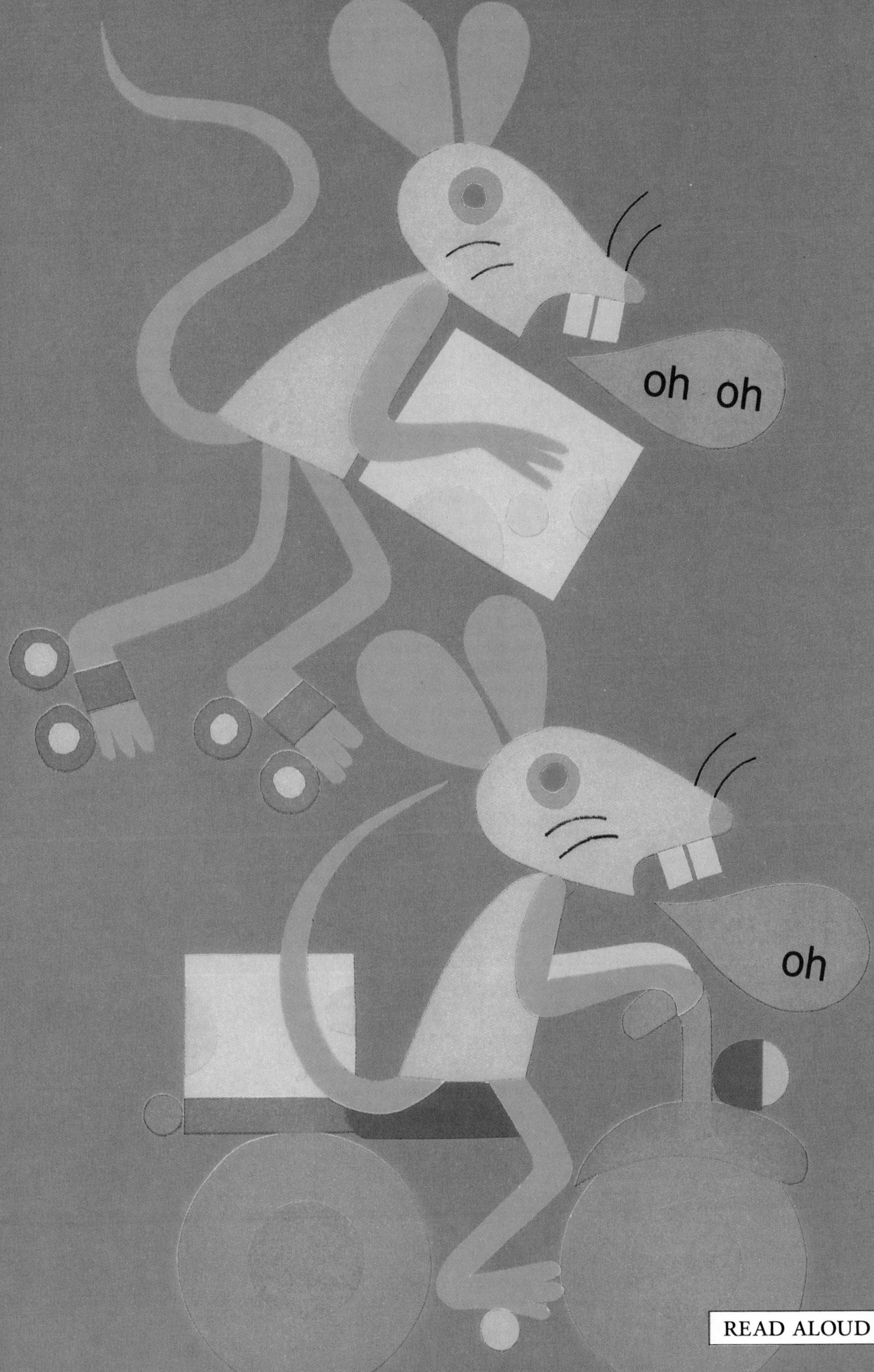

READ ALOUD

Some words are fancy words.

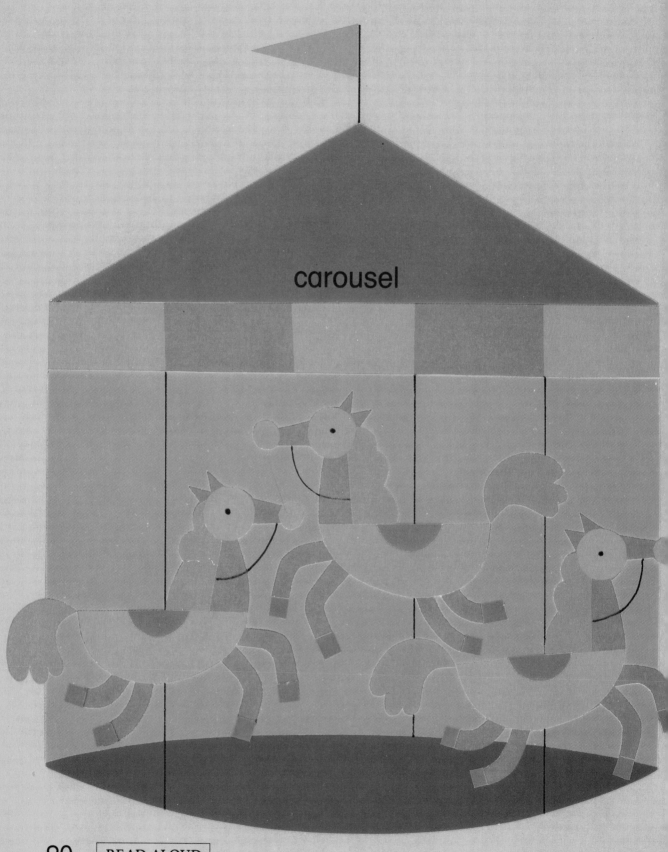

carousel

READ ALOUD

poodle

delicatessen

Some words are dancy words.

hula hoop

READ ALOUD

hokeypokey

ballet

Some words are prancy words.

tango

cakewalk

READ ALOUD

strut

cheerleader

Some words are antsy words.

jelly

jelly

READ ALOUD

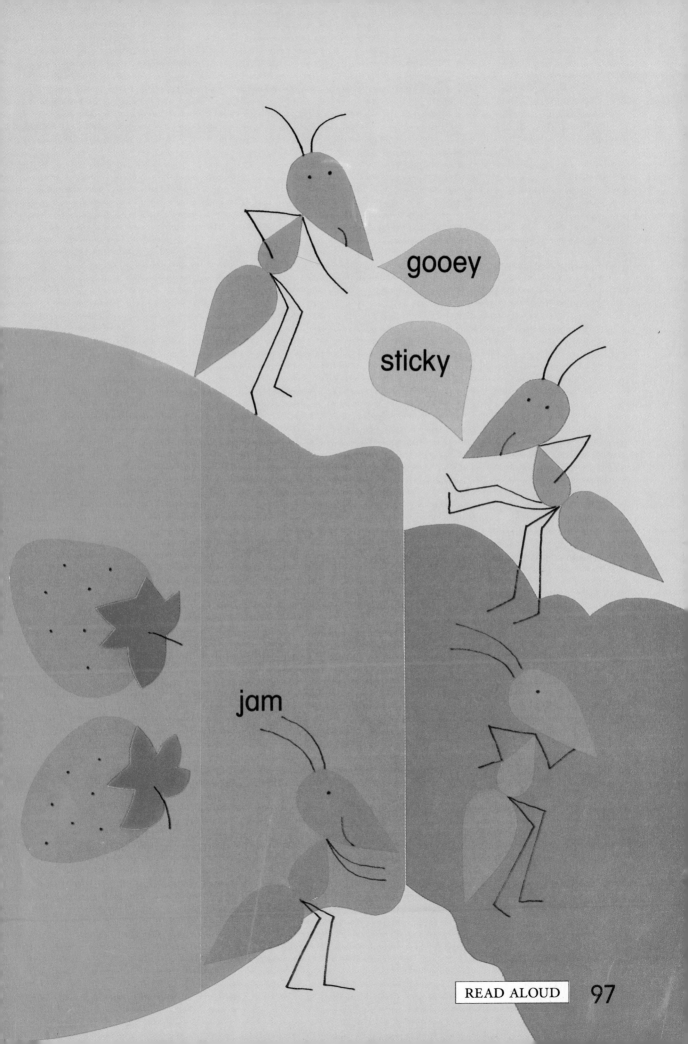

Some words are fancy, dancy, prancy, antsy words.

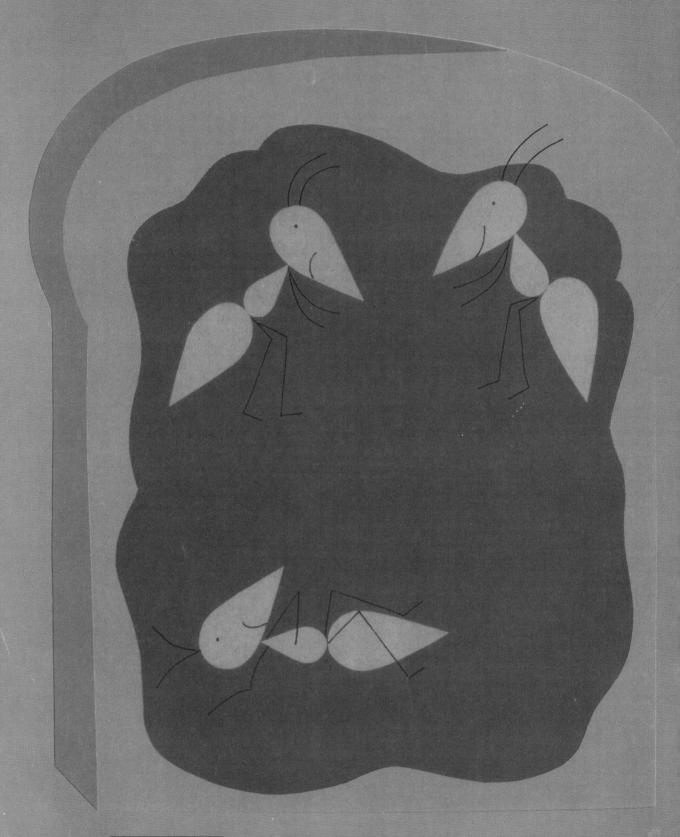

READ ALOUD

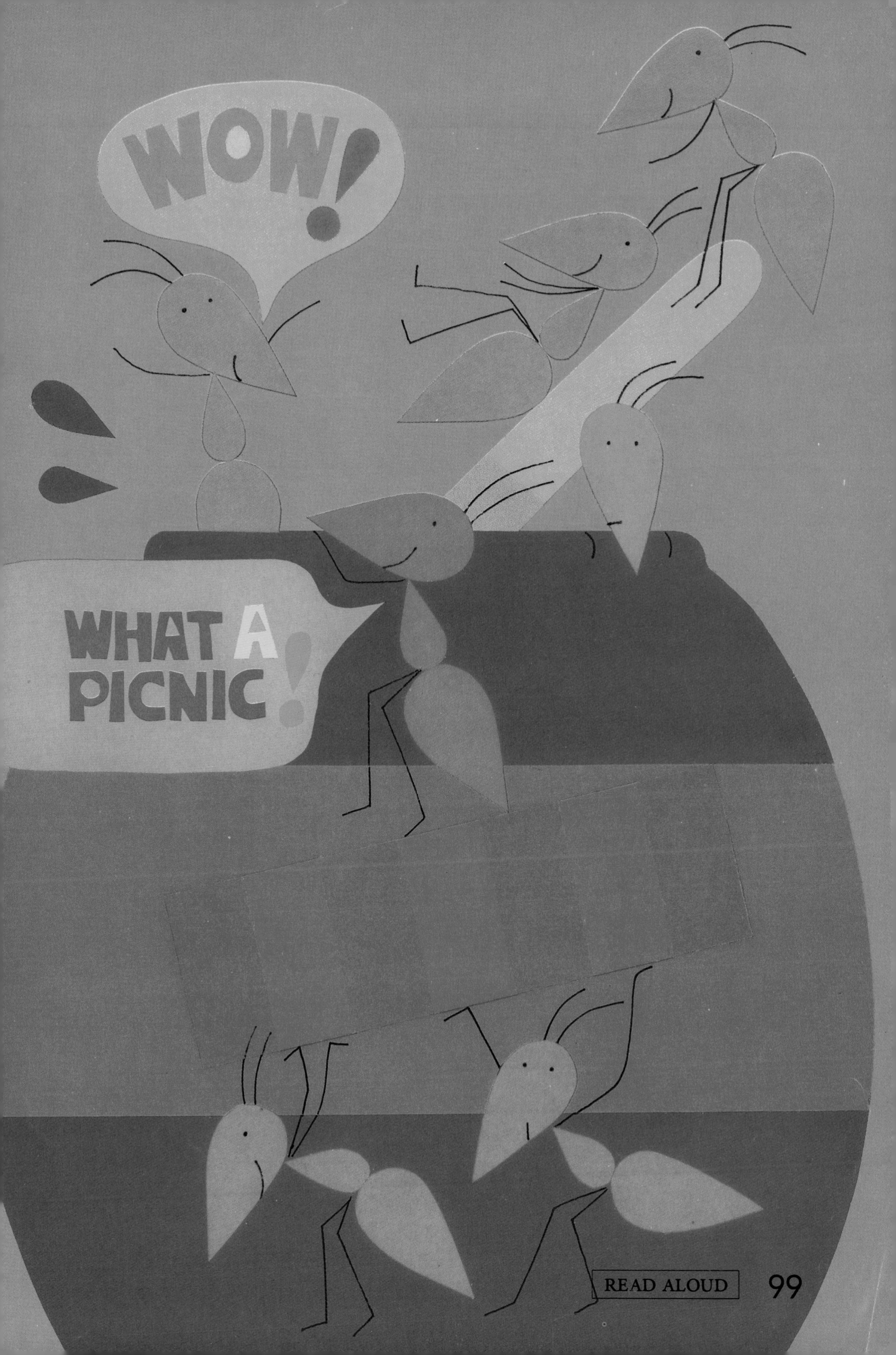
WOW!
WHAT A PICNIC!

ABOUT THE
Authors & Illustrators

Jose Aruego

Jose Aruego illustrated *whose mouse are you?* When he was little, he liked funny pictures and cartoons. You can tell he likes funny little animals when you look at his books. The next time you are in the library, look for funny animals in more of his books, like *Leo the Late Bloomer.*

Mirra Ginsburg

Mirra Ginsburg grew up far away in
Russia. When she was little, she loved the
stories Russian children were told. Even
today, she collects stories told to children
all over the world. *Across the Stream* is a
children's story from her collection.

Robert Kraus

Robert Kraus started out by drawing cartoons. He even won an award for one of his cartoons when he was eleven years old. Then he decided to write children's books. One of those books is *whose mouse are you?*

David McCord

David McCord grew up on a ranch in Oregon. His poems often tell about things he did as a boy. His poem, "Song of the Train," sounds like a train moving along the tracks.